D1568232

MILES PRESS

Indiana University South Bend Department of English

OUR

LIST

OF

SOLUTIONS

42 Miles Press
Editor, David Dodd Lee
Copyright© 2011 Carrie Oeding. All rights reserved.
ISBN 978-0-9830747-1-7 (pbk. alk. paper)

For permission, required to reprint or broadcast more than several lines, write to:
42 Miles Press, Department of English, Indiana University South Bend
1700 Mishawaka Avenue, South Bend, IN 46615

http://42miles.wordpress.com

Art Direction, Tricia Hennessy, Design, Jennie Nusbaum, Production, Paul Sizer
The Design Center, Frostic School Of Art, Western Michigan University.
Printing, McNaughton & Gunn, Inc.

OUR LIST OF SOLUTIONS

POEMS BY CARRIE OEDING

10/30/19

For Jane and Wally, Wally and Jane

CONTENTS

I.

What good are insights? They only make things worse.

—Raymond Carver

*Maybe I'm here to dispel the illusion that life
proceeds smoothly as long as one pays attention.*

—Claire Bateman

ALL MY FRIENDS' BARBECUES NEED ATTENDING

I'm not as much to look at as I think I am.

It is the fashion to put oneself down, except when fishing.

Someone hands me a plate of Mexican potato salad and says, *Who made this fusion crap?*

My friends say, *We love you! Don't be so hard on yourself*. I keep moving toward the edge of the pool to see my nice ears.

Friends! In order to have them I must say I let old people through doors first, that babies' shrieks make me gently call my breasts "momma," that every girl loves a pony, and that I think two lovers are broken halves that make a whole.

I'll mention Rob's name. Rob. Rob says he'd rather go fishing than come to these barbecues. I agree. Rob and I aren't friends.

The real moment of each night is when I decide between *I have trees for friends* or *I have friends for trees.*

When I'm ready to tell a story, I will. When I am, back off.

The best decision, when preparing to go, always is to make the Mexican potato salad.

The wrong decision, when accepting an invitation, is to admit I know that a separated couple, a deviated septum, and a three-fingered child are still not as bad as being the shy one in the group.

Trees. Trees! The overlooked meat!

I'd prefer to hate myself than just say I hate myself.

My friends say I don't mention my friends enough. Give us names!

And when it's time to say goodnight, someone calls me *Joan.*

HIS LIST OF SOLUTIONS

Tonight, again, all the neighbors are in his kitchen.

There is a reason why his
heart droops heavy like his suspended pots and pans
but only one of them knows why.

He's sure they'll never leave without him
they will pull back the wall panels   release
        the smell of every soup he's made them
                stay and trace each of themselves on his sheets
    point out his devotion in the dog's wag   take his door.

No, they're only taking down his whiskey
(an easy party) a bit of bread. No, no
never has he demanded better friends
                                    or a chicken when the oven's empty.
    After six whiskeys he can't tell which neighbor can see through him.

Without seven he can't tell the night what he doesn't see.

The faintest smell— noodles, broth   no meat.

Where is she, who is the one he couldn't mistake
who'd mistake herself for something he needs?

If his water burns   if his whiskey boils   if he breaks
his hand while pulling a piece of bread   yet someone (she!) insists   eat and drink
then he will know which one is the one who could come over alone

(she will leave when he asks)

could bring the chicken

                         (she will never leave)

could build a reason for him to enjoy that one soup he will never perfect

                                        (she will anger and stir).

She'll feel inadequately for the both of them

and hang the pots back up before he refuses to dry them

and the neighborhood will keep falling

for his open door.

WE LIKE STEVE AND LOUISE'S LOVE

Abby's attempts at dying
are nothing like Loretta's.
Abby likes a push, open-ended notes,
and knowing we know she's tried before, but tells us
she can never decide
on a final face to think of while she dies.
Loretta
only chooses pills
with tea, pills with tea.
We have all these stupid choices,
but Steve and Louise don't need to choose.
They have traded fortunes, exchanged reasons to live,
sworn oaths to never leave
without first dying or chaining the dog outside,
and found each other.
Steve has a tattoo which says *Angie*
so Louise would love him more.
Louise imagines a child too angel-cheeked
for Steve (or, if needed, for her) to leave.
One of them burns hard for saying
love 7,459 times in the period of a marriage or maybe it was a meal.
Their love is like not choosing to die of a reason,
their love is like saying *That's heavy* without laughing (please, someone giggle).
Although their love is no secret, we'd say it's like
whispering to a hush-hush lover *They're all going to hate us,*
or like loving someone
yet still wanting to. Like,
like, like—

Please, someone, what is the time? What happened to Loretta?

Please, someone,
throw rocks at us or something. Stop us.
There's something better
we should be doing (Oh, but they throw the good parties).
Isn't there someone's life we could be saving (Once an underwear party!)?

Please,
close our blinds on Louise and Steve's picnics
and the way they make us want hurt in love and not
whatever love would be without fear of loss, or at least
without fear of saying the same thing over and over.

Yes, watching them may make us want to uncover
a tattoo of our name on someone's young but aging ass
(oh how we heart *time's winged chariot*),
but somebody, somebody,
like your whimpering real dog more than a love-saving baby,
like the taste of your cake heart,
like the empty space behind your swing, start pumping.
Don't just like the lack of choice
in who you could really love, like all the choices
you could make to *avoid* love in hopes of finding love.
Find their romance wine, steal it, yes and toast
to what you still haven't found,
show yourself, shake it on the corner.
                              We want to look out our windows again.

JOY

I wish it wasn't dancing
that gave me joy—
the way the first step needs a sister step,
one we'd desert for a man who says *Gotcha!*
Let's make him ugly, let's twist our ankles.

Oh dumb legs, silly pregnant music,
stupid empty space between dancing bodies that longs not to be space.
Dancing is one way to have joy.
Someone says it is the best, it is the only joy, as he dips me
and we continue to dance.
No one is dipped seriously by her dance partner.
Can't there be something different about this joy, my joy?
Throw in a shotgun with this rhythm, some fishy water, a plate of cheese.
Can't there be something besides dancing,
or maybe can't there be something besides joy?
Oh, can't there be something besides joy?

Someone find the someone who said dancing is the best form of joy,
he's moved to a new partner, and tell him he's wrong.
Someone find someone who wants to find anyone
and tell them no one wants to be found.

This whole time someone's been singing
a song about lovemaking,
and I should listen, sure, because it's something to do besides dance.
But why does a person need something to do?
The making is joy, no, the making is love.
And all around we're bound to be punished
like someone dancing who doesn't want to touch ground.

La di, la di, la di do. Sing to me like you could never give me joy.

And if everything is aspiring to be music—
the making and the dancing and the joying,
if they all are dying to be music,
why does music just get to be music?

Music,
I can beat you too.
There has to be something even better than you.
I'm sorry but I'm gonna have to sit down,
no, I'm gonna leave, drive, drive so the wind in my
broken window that won't roll up is louder than any song on lovemaking.
I'll keep one hand out the window
and one on a shotgun that I'd never own,
yes, no hands steering.
Perhaps some day I won't figure out what it is
about my open hand that makes me smile.

SANDY SAYS *NO MORE!* TO JUST ABOUT EVERYTHING

She just picked a morning and waited
for the sky to turn dark, and when it did
the stars had no choice.
She looked up and told them they weren't in her life anymore.

Sappy, silent tick tock of night,
glorified dots people tattoo to their intended skin,
the bright excuse lovers on the beach give at night
for pressing sand between each other and their stupid *yeses,*
stagnant sign that the apocalypse was thought of,
childish reason to *oooh.*
Silly stars, she has cut you out of her life, what can you undo?

No, you don't know each other anymore.
You always tell the same stories about yourself.
She is done waiting for your bastards to fall, and tired
of clear nights. Thunderstorms, she likes—
the light of lightning which strikes
and is over itself.

It may be hard
but she has discovered sunglasses at night.
Sandy keeps busy—
she is recently quite sexy after sundown.
Men who hate astronomy are fond of her.
Yes she is full of choices, even though she does not believe in them.

Most of you have burned cold already, there is no need to see your ghost.

And so Sandy
had it out for a moment with the stars.
Some things you just don't have a say in, she explained,
then quickly went inside to let them leave, to let the sunrise take her side.

THE WOMEN WEAR BLACK

even in the sun.
You wonder
if they're hip, sullen . . . oh no— hard to get?
You think they mourn
because they sleep with each other's husbands and lovers,
cover each other with gossip and glares,
raise their glasses and clink to another day
that they have spared each other, clink
to another day when they will *not* spare each other
when a man's hands tear off one woman's black.
The women are not ready to say why they wear black.
They wear black while not having fun.
They know Saturday nights that are see-through, ripped, tight with fur.
They know to go to church in the morning,
but they still wear black to pray
that God is *not* a woman
and wonder how She is settling with a heaven full of men.
The women are not ready to whisper *Amen*.
They are not ready to shout out sins.
They're too busy undressing their men.
The women are not ready to say why they wear black.
They do not know what else to dress themselves in.
But at night when they whisper to one another,
never
and never settle,
only then do they know what to wear.
But the sun rises
and heaven exists only in the light, during a day that is not theirs.
Girls, we need sunglasses.
Our squinting has blurred us into a glob of *we*.
How will we ever know one from another?
How can we call out naked shouts of *Delia, Mary, Bernadine?*
Women, wear black and laugh,
so I know which way to walk.
Oh boys and men, I'm sorry,
my back turning has nothing to do with you.

THOSE WOMEN ARE LAUGHING

Sorry Susanna,
we've already worn the red dress
tight, yes, without a slip,
once with the zipper broken,
to a wedding and to our birthday,
where, yes, we ate the cake with our hands.
We ate the dress.
We wore it as if we had a secret,
over and over and Friday and Sunday,
until, silly Susanna, there never was a dress.

Sorry, we've already demanded
the cake and the gun and the empty room.
But go ahead and say it
if you think you can pretend.
We've always been loud.

Sorry Susanna,
we've already slept with him, each one of us,
and told him, "There won't be anyone
'like me,' 'like me,' 'like me,'"
and walked away refusing to make him better,
you're not the first one. Yes,
aren't we just something.

Do you whisper, *I can do this better*,
Susanna? Funny how we knew that.
We've already done better.

We've already seen you, Susanna.
Yes, and? We see you.

But I'm different.
Yep, we've said that. Made that true. It is true.

Oh, we've done that too, yes,
been true, been right, been dead once or twice,
yes we've even died and come back
in the red dress they buried us in.

Yes, go if you want.
We'll understand, we already do.
We *are* loud, we can be.
That is nothing new.
We realize how funny we are, how loud, how we talk
sleep, wash, aim.
Or, yes you can stay and wait and laugh. What comes
is always better than before, sure.
Someone will come who can make us laugh.
It's a shame she will be just like you, like you, like you.

APOLOGY TO MEDITATION

The meditation teacher said he wants to leave you alone with me. There should be no third party between me and "existence."

The meditation teacher said I would soon understand the nature of the mind rather than fight with it. He winked at me then, a bit creepy. I'll be honest, he really didn't, but it's my nature to say quick things to try and make it interesting. Winking is totally predictable.

My friend Jen would like to get to know you because she wants to stay in the moment.

I don't want to get into it with her, but there could be a moment of a bright autumn tree, or a bright autumn tree that leads me to notice crows, cats, dents in my car, cars on my cat, leaves shaped like cats, the world is cruel. And then it's not— bright autumn trees that come alive and wink. Or trees which then, suddenly, suddenly suddenly I notice then what happens next?   Looking looking   where's the moment I'm in?   Bright autumn trees that don't notice me.

I'm not going back to class to find out how to look at a leaf or who really winked.

I got to know someone once and it led to third parties.

Dear bright autumn trees, surprise me.

Dear meditation, I'm sorry, I know I am getting you all wrong— but now you know how a person can feel and why they wouldn't want to let that go.

MORE WAYS TO SAY *ELOISE*

I.

I can't think of Eugene without Eloise.
My lover is sad too.
When he sleeps next to me I roll over
and ask, *Why are you crying?*
He waits and sniffs
and then I hear, *Yes*.
I let him be, who wants to talk about it?
I dream of a past lover, Jim,
rollerblading around me while I eat in a courtyard.
Eloise is dead,
Eugene . . . who can think of him?
I think of Eloise and I
I say, *you*, but I think I'm just pretending to say it.
I dream of Jim more and more—
rollerblading by while I spoon gelato
and I remind myself I cut him out of my life.
Eloise is dead and I can't bring myself to see Eugene,
but I can sleep next to my lover.
What would he think if I told him of Jim?

II.

Perhaps Eloise knows now
who she was to me.
Damn, maybe she would never know
if I didn't think of her after she died.
It's not that I care
what she knows of herself in my head,
but what could she possibly know?
In my kitchen I pick up a mango,

Eloise, Eloise, but perhaps she didn't come back
as this fruit. Maybe she's in the water I drink
and the way I swallow talks to her or
reveals how I really feel about water.
Have some real emotions!
my lover pleads, walking through the room.
Perhaps— Eloise is in him!
He's left the kitchen before I can reach her.
Maybe she's reaching for me right now.
There's a mango on the floor.
Outside a neighbor walks her Husky
and I never imagined Eloise would come back
as the only dog I call out to.

III.

I can't think of how to feel now
so I will think of Eloise right now. I think of Eloise
right now so I won't know how to feel.
I'm bothered by the whole world right now,
and even though she's dead they expect me
to still say her name.

IV.

Someone asks how I'm doing.
Someone asks how I'm doing.
Isn't she dead? I ask.
They hand me cups of black tea.
I haven't thought of anything except Eugene.
My lover breaks my teacup for me.
My lover buys me a dog.
I'm sure I would have cut her out of my life anyway.

NEIGHBOR CURSE

Thanks for never using the garden tools
I loaned you, which you never returned.
I've been watching.
You won't have any tomatoes this summer.

Thanks for being so nice to my dog.
I saw you slip her treats
so one of us would like you.

Thanks for having no tomatoes this summer.
I would've trained my dog to eat them.

Even though you don't have a wife
for my wife to know, thanks
for getting to know my wife.
I know you'll try to have her
slip off her useless garden clogs
and walk a little softer on your floors.

A lot, a lot, of thanks—
I won't have any tomatoes this summer.

Thank you— for I trust myself. I had a hunch about you,
and loaned you the garden tools
so you'd prove me right.

STORM'S A'COMIN

Friends, we are not asking for the story, let's put our best hats on

as everyone is asking for trouble, no, for pineapple to be exotic fruit again.

We all know what happened to Dean,

and the afternoon clouds are just asking for trouble.

So there's a story about Dean and one

about a funny hat, a favorite hat flying off in the wind,

even though the storm hasn't come yet.

Someone's mom has gout or a goat— it's hard to hear above the wind.

Maureen and Steve were married.

Darrell and Louise were married.

Maureen and Steve had a house, had no money,

so both couples shared the home and soon traded spouses.

We knew it would happen because Maureen liked pineapple.

Now Maureen and Darrell

and Louise and Steve . . . ah . . .

Who cares if it's realistic or not?

If you really care you're asking for trouble.

Darrell cares about what will happen to his beach house he can't afford to build.

Either Steve or Louise cares, yes he or she really does.

No, the afternoon clouds aren't asking for trouble, they're *gonna be* trouble.

Dean's leaving town, there isn't a reason;

Tallahassee is having its worst tropical storm since 1993,

but we all know why he's really gone.

No one wonders where Amy is—

we know she's on the pier waiting for the wind to be a story.

Oh Amy, how many times have we heard your tales

of how close you've come to death!

She loves to shout to the not-yet storm, *You don't know what's gonna happen either!*

Such words, Amy, such words you can use,

but where's the story? Where is Dean? He's never heard of Amy

but how he pines for her back turned against the yet-to-be-hit land.

Somewhere Dean is forever driving from Florida, not thinking of the storm,

but shaking his head, *That's the way things go, that's the way,*

just singing this song that's like a song, but not one really.

I HAVE BEEN IN MORE UNCOMFORTABLE SITUATIONS THAN THIS

To the next person who dislikes me,
let me say it's true a person needs enemies,
and I'm sure you could be a great one,
one who thinks of insults while ironing silk,
one who is never wrinkled.
I'm sure I could stick it to you,
since I'm funny and you're not,
since I can scowl better than a barbecue grill.
Listen, Katherine tells me about her enemies.
She says they're like sweat in a Carolina summer,
spilling down your skin when you pick up a Coke.
She says sometimes they're more fun than eating chips.
She grins and says, *Soon one will come around*
for you, like my teeth rounding this apple.
The best apple I ever had was like having perfect teeth, it was like
comparing an apple to something instead of fucking eating it.
I'm guilty— I compare things to you, too.
You could be a person or you could be an apple.
You could scorn me quicker than cavities.
I don't want to place insults next to you,
I want to think of a celery stalk and say you are like it,
but not in an insulting way,
and just think about it for awhile—
You are a sliver,
you are a chessboard,
you are a trampoline, you are—
I don't know, but I say this all to stall awhile,
I say this all with my barbecue scowl that's now a grin.
You are outside my house about to ring.
I am standing in my bathroom brushing my teeth.
Before you touch my doorbell and before we meet,
I should feel something for you
because I still can,
and I think I can't go anywhere and neither can you.

A LOOK ABOUT MONTY

Nobody said you had to marry it, or me. Yes, I'm attractive. One day, for instance, you will feel like starting over. Everyone else is in this together. They can have me. They can tell me, *Monty, nothing's missing*. They can pretend something is. Enough not to know. I'll last until they decide I noticed them first. I walk all over town. They say first the head, then the body will follow.

The first time I saw Miranda she said she'd been following me for months. No, she said this later. I said, *It's not you*. This time, I meant it. You could find yourself considered. The next time I saw Miranda she looked terrible. Like she came in with a draft. She said I looked good.

One day, for instance, you could find yourself unheard of. One year I spent never looking at myself. So far, I'm all face. Few, probably, have noticed you. Your choice. You don't have to stand in the way. You don't have to stand unnoticed. This is not a wedding day.

As if there were always something to work towards. An event. A conflict. A day when you admit what you first thought of me.

MORNING SONG FOR THE PORCH LIGHT

Still on, you greet the sun with your uselessness, or perhaps the sun greets you with it, showing you once again that you should have been turned off before now when even the moths have left and soon the wasps will come out only to try to get inside my windows. Morning's not your time of day. Sorry. Surely my electric bill is rising from night after night. I blush, or at least think of flinching, that this is the best I can think of, to leave you on because of a little twitch and strain of my legs while falling awake each time I feel I stopped breathing or I'm being watched, then in the morning speak of you insincerely, call it a song, and now wonder how much the wasp will hurt.

I wish I could say I leave you on all night because I'm a sham. I want all the neighbors to think the light is on for a good reason, a casual reason, a reason as everyday as a reason to put on pants, casual pants.

I wish I could say I leave you on because I'm cold, because I can, because I've never cried while reading a story, except once I did, yet at that time I would've cried anyway, or maybe it's that the story was about me.

I wish I could say I leave you on because I love to be right. I know what's good for you and all the porch lights should join you, but then I'd have to make up a reason for why this is true. People do, people do.

This isn't a song for you, this isn't a song. A song is something for mating or marring. Or maybe something to just get you out of bed. Those morning birds I sometimes hate, now they have something to sing about. So what, they do every day. God, somebody sting me and get it over with. If I were cold I wouldn't worry about such things, I'd never get close enough to be stung. And if I were also a sham I could hide this fact and pretend to be pensive or pretend to be mysterious, whatever's the fashion. And if I were right, oh you get the idea. It's so easy to be right.

All night no one needed you to be helped up the stairs. No one slinked by and decided to break into unlit homes instead. No one stumbled past and wondered if the moans were loud or quiet from the lovers inside. No one hoped someone's bed on this street wasn't half empty. Oh, that's a sad one.

It's morning. Last night I slept. Not as much as the night before, so tonight the kitchen light will join you. Then who knows. I'll catch one of those morning birds, force it to sing all night to stave off however fear needs staving, or make it never want to sing again. And if I were a different person I could think maybe today was the day I'd meet someone who could tell me that's a terrible thought to have, then touch me on the shoulder in a way I thought I hated, but I prefer a song with a singer who really means it.

This really is a morning song, not quite for you or me, but it is a song. I'm not going to say it's just the best I can do because this is no consolation. This isn't a song that's trying to be a better song, trying to aspire to be a song with a full bed and rested mornings, not a song about what it one morning will be. Thank you for staying on all night and while I know you're just a light, you didn't burn out, but if you had the morning would still begin, thank you thank you, with you being just a light.

SANDY'S BEAUTY

One of my neighbors said, *You're* beautiful!
as if she discovered Beautiful for me,
led me to its doorstep,
as if I was searching for the doorbell of
Ugly, Spark-less, or some guy named Roy who says I lose.
And now my neighbor has introduced me to Beautiful.
Hello Beautiful.
What do you like? It's almost winter.
Beautiful, they say you and I have not met before.
Do you think you're better than snow?
Frankly Beautiful,
I have always had a feeling about myself.
Would my neighbor believe me?
What do you like?
I'd like to confirm that we have never met—
Loosen your tie, unzip your skirt,
move into the neighborhood.
Snow will come, I don't have a shovel.

ROY'S BLUE SHIRTS

Finding things was even more tiring
than looking for them.

First he found Sara who said there was nothing to him
but blue eyes and he had to start looking again.

Now when he looked for things
he forgot what he had ever found.

He was tired but he was quite a looker
so when he found one blue shirt he bought more.

Now every day he wears one (with those eyes!).
Every day we know him by it: *Hey it's Roy Blue-Shirt!*

Chin up, being known by a shirt is easier than looking
for a memorable face. Now that he wore blue shirts

everything else could go by.
He had the blue shirts and they weren't really him.

Whoever else he wasn't could strut in and out, stay if it wanted.
And any reason everyone made for why he always wore blue,

well, they'd be making up who he was too—
Oh, that silly Blue-Shirt!   It never found him grumpy.

But grumpiness found him
alone and refusing to ask to be left as such

and it got messy— blue shirts, grumpiness, no Sara,
so he got rid of the blue shirts and yes, missed them.

No, no.   He would be grumpy
he would wear a blue shirt every day. Enough.

But now came Sara down the street whom
he neither looked for nor found,

holding hands with blue-eyed Dan.

AMY WEARS BLUE SHIRTS EVERY DAY, TOO

I won't ask you, Amy, what everyone else does.
I don't care to know if you wear blue
because Roy always wears blue.

Oh hell, even I can't get away
without mentioning him.
Please, don't think I am like everyone else.

As if anyone could have anything
to do with the way you make your own table
with only one chair.
You smile at your own blue.
The way you never seem
to watch anyone

makes me wonder if you
were the first one
to wear blue.

You are always alone,
and I'd like to think somehow

when you wear blue
you're better than Amy,
you kiss the back of your own hand,
you're wearing red, black, all of it too,
you're breaking your own heart,
and it inspires me to wear blue, no,

to talk to Roy,
ask him why he wears blue,
then do blue better than anyone,
and I'll make my own table, too.
Better, without chairs.

TRYING TOO HARD

It is one of the many things you do wrong.
But, we'll start out in another direction, a sort of surprise
(You like surprises, don't you? You want it fresh
fresh fresh, unexpected as plaid with plaid!).
So we'll begin with criticizing your friends
instead of you. Oh, wrong wrong you.

Your friend Stacey loves language, she says she says.
Cultivated corollaries— Say it, it's just like living!
Discovering words is like finding chocolate goats
in your basket instead of mere bunnies.
She finds a *suture* summoning.
Persimmon over and over.

What's a more exotic fruit to say? You'll find out,
and steal her high heels.

And then there's Ted. He can see—
Look— time waits for a handshake.
See— honey is no longer honey.
I am beside you when you fall, and then fall some more!
You are un-flailing trees. Angels! Angels!

You can imagine bees better than he, no? Visions? No problem.

And there are more friends. We're going to stop. We have a date,
you understand.

If we are wrong about any of this, please,
set us out to melt.

We can't decide which one of you
(you! your friends!) tries harder
to be you and not you.
You hollow out a place at home, in your bed,
hunker down to think of how to fire out
the best angel-less vision or way to peel oranges
at Tracey, sorry, *Stacey* or Ted or or—

Lovers fall into your bed and you hold tight
to the bedding afraid they'll steal your thunder
instead of your heart (they can have that line!).
But in the loosened sheets each one has seen
you stitch a night with your ordinary rhythm,
sleeping as anyone does,
even the sigh. And yet, and yet,
we do think there was something genuine in it.

SANDY, WILL YOU QUIT SAYING SUCH THINGS?

This is what everyone tells me, but

when I want to be blinded, don't show up in pastel.

Don't give me your perfect homemade cake

when I want better.

Don't tell me, *Oh Sandy, I know you hope.*

A lover told you that you were the beautiful child

but never saw a picture—

Don't wait for me to point out how people work.

Your friends will leave you for a stranger's birthday,

and you'll never get over it. I can't wait

to tell you how your kitten will turn out.

Oh, I'm ruining everything.

Go,

get angry at what I'm saying to avoid me—

yes, even your anger is too light.

You have such promise to be like everyone else.

My little princes and dolls, how could I ever

break that sweet tooth of yours?

What have I done? What have I done? This

is what I could ask myself if you ever listened

(How that would feel!)

and then stopped asking me if I enjoy anything.

Yes,

you misunderstand everything I ask.

Don't you understand why I can't call it hope?

Let's get you a soda,

with two straws and one person

to love, who'd break your cake, cut your heart

and its songs of what a heart is.

Then maybe you can come over

and surprise me with something better,

something that I would really

never get over, something that would ruin us both.

COMING IN FROM THE GARDEN WHILE I THINK OF GOING BACK

Will it come to me when I am gone   what I shouldn't have planted   where the thistle
could be hiding   where the edge is to stand and admire best   or what of it isn't mine
It is better to leave   simply   Return without confusion of why I complicate
It is better to stay too long and realize you can never   stay too long   work too hard at
leaving   in order to come back and feel this   is the better day to be in the garden

I started with daisies   they were the best daisies   I could do better than them
         so I planted some flowers I wonder if I ever knew the name of
It doesn't matter   I knew they were the best   Who knows if they were even really
daisies at first   but I have so many now and they are the best
                                                      so good they could only be better

I scattered the seeds to make them look wild   I like rows of flowers
                    clean rows   I know I can plant neatly   so I don't   didn't don't
Daisies are too easy   but I let them stay to remind me of what is

There was the season with the first daisies   then I wanted to know how I did so well
   then the season of better flowers and expected vegetables   How was this my making
      Then I was no longer gardener   host   patient   I can do better than patience
I started with the season   but when I wanted to keep planting   beyond it   I couldn't
Worried that nothing in it would surprise me   I have to obey the season's length   outcome
It is better I included toys   shoes and   and   To plant them in the garden than to take
   a garden seriously   I could quickly return   and return   Return with a shirt left by
the last neighbor to visit   Let's see how this will refuse to grow

 Why did I begin why did I begin   I don't want to ask   Oh beginnings

Does it stay with me   Do I have to now think about how   I've been changed
It's easy to supply what was supposed to happen   I should've become soft
been present   been full of dirt   become beautiful as if it had never been done before
Silly silly silly   I know how to squint at the sight of beauty   but I can't give in to

simple welcomes   without thinking how it is made   it could be better
                 Beauty   It's true I don't know if I want such acceptance

Quickly   I will take another look at what it needs   what I can't provide

Please I   am winning something   and with hope it's something I'd never choose to want
but still could grow   win   in neat rows   but only if I want it in such ways
        I started I started   How it could be better is only found in failure
Endurance isn't needed when you don't know what you're holding out for
I can never unplant   only ruin   It would be best to go back now   Now now
I am afraid of what will occur to me   (the now the now)   with these hands out of the dirt
                        When will the slugs and aphids come

That's not a cross look, it's a sign of life, but I'm glad you care how I look at you.

—Frank O'Hara

PRELUDE TO HOW THE WORLD WORKS

I.

Envy the list, its certainty of what's needed in the To-do.

Its reason for being read. Its reason for being, read.

Its shape as known as a sidewalk. Its form lacking face and resembling

the unnaturally natural lines of an Andy Goldsworthy.

Its line determined not to be a fence, a contra dance, a zipper

on my sequined skirt, each sequin getting its moment to be seen.

Its inability to hold one item. Like the eye chart.

The list envies the eye chart.

No need to see what it means.

II.

What makes spiders stick to their webs?

Have you ever eaten a chicken omelet?

If I teach my dog to do *shake* with his hind legs, is it a hello or goodbye?

How far away can you live and still be my neighbor?

When was your first blush?

What is the opposite of a knock?

Do bugs sneeze?

What makes me look like my dog or my dog look like me?
        If I adopt a cute dog, will I grow more attractive or will my dog lose her looks?

What country is this birthmark? Who will invade?

What's the safest way to swerve, crash, and avoid that deer?

        How long can you hold out? How long can you hold?

Children of botoxed mothers, what facial expressions will you acquire?

Do you see sunspots? A moment without love? A love that demands it's a love?

Look at me when I'm talking to you—
                How far can you be while this command remains a reasonable demand
in that unreasonable way that's reasonable?

Puzzled faces: why always the question on our faces instead of the face on our questions?

III.

Look, a face!

Look, a face!

Look, a face! Look, a face! Look, a face! Look, a face! Look, a face! Look, a face! Look, a face!
Look, a face! Look, a face! Look, a face! Look, a face! Look, a face! Look, a face! Look, a face!
Look, a face! Look, a face! Look, a face! Look, a face! Look, a face! Look, a face! Look, a face!
Look, a face! Look, a face! Look, a face! Look, a face! Look, a face! Look, a face! Look, a face!
Look, a face! Look, a face! Look, a face! Look, a face! Look, a face! Look, a face! Look, a face!
Look, a face! Look, a face! Look, a face! Look, a face! Look, a face! Look, a face! Look, a face!
Look, a face! Look, a face! Look, a face! Look, a face! Look, a face! Look, a face! Look, a face!
Look, a face! Look, a face! Look, a face! Look, a face! Look, a face! Look, a face! Look, a face!
Look, a face! Look, a face! Look, a face! Look, a face! Look, a face! Look, a face! Look, a face!
Look, a face! Look, a face! Look, a face! Look, a face! Look, a face! Look, a face! Look, a face!
Look, a face! Look, a face! Look, a face! Look, a face! Look, a face! Look, a face! Look, a face!
Look, a face! Look, a face! Look, a face! Look, a face! Look, a face! Look, a face! Look, a face!
Look, a face! Look, a face! Look, a face! Look, a face! Look, a face! Look, a face! Look, a face!
Look, a face! Look, a face! Look, a face! Look, a face! Look, a face! Look, a face! Look, a face!
Look, a face! Look, a face! Look, a face! Look, a face! Look, a face!

Look, a face!

Look, a face!

Look, a face!

IV.

You'll look at faces, first. You'll cry in the crib and a face will come, and cry and a face. Really it's a presence and it presents itself, your eyes and focus not sharp enough, not ready to really see anything, but you need someone and that someone comes. You won't really look at all, but will remember being received. A body will be like a face, and looking will be being seen. When you're older, this will be a memory not a memory of an image.

                         Yet, you try to remember it as if it is one.

You'll look for faces, first. Whatever the composition, line, direction, color, faces always dominate an image, a scene.

       First for the face in the stone, before the stone in her face. The winking house, before seeing faces locking their doors. Then everything's a face, after much seeing of faces.

I look because of faces. I do a lot of looking away. Pretending not to look. Everything's too sincere after so much pretending. Everything's looking after a lot of looking away. The spoon on the counter says it's dirty or I need to eat or you were sick on Friday and here's the stain of medicine. I am seen by objects. Pick me up. I've been waiting. Throw me away. Keep me.

                  I take off my gloves to touch your doorbell. I wouldn't shake hands with my gloves on. I take my gloves off when I ring your doorbell and say a little thank you to my cluttered kitchen.

V.

A lot of us will continue to rely on, *Hey, you were in my dream last night,*
never admitting we pulled down our bra strap, it didn't fall.
We left our shoelace untied and we're trying not to trip. Point us out.

I want to make something beautiful out of the everyday.

This thing here, I use it every day.
It is the everyday, then.

Here's this thing I don't use but it's always around, and here I am noticing that I've been overlooking
it.

Here is this thing you said was beautiful. It was made by someone else. And here is something that
just exists. And it too is called beautiful.

How did you know that? How do you know everything?

VI.

MEMO: Answers for Sandy

TO: Sandy
FROM: The Department of Applicable Answers
Re: How the World Works

A: Spiders only touch webs with the tips of their legs, which they constantly clean with their mouths. The main spokes of the web are made of dry silk.

A: Eleven minutes for medium eggs. Thirteen for large eggs [boiling].

A: A thickening agent found in food, such as the Wendy's Frosty, is made of kelp.

A: Sometimes garlic turns blue when you cook it with lemon. This is not supposed to happen.

A: Scientists have recently photographed wild gorillas having sex face-to-face.

A: Just smelling the aroma of coffee is enough to change the activity of rats' genes.

A: You should ask for it.

A: The agent in Pepto that turns your tongue black is bismuth subsalicylate. It mixes with sulfur in your spit.

A: Haystacks in Australia are spontaneously combusting at high rates.

A: My dad was a bee-keeper.

A: Woodchucks and groundhogs are the same animal, but I think one sounds made up.

A: Avoid plastic ones.

A: Avoid the salad bar.

A: I saw that, too.

A: Whales. The Moby Dick kind.

A: I can't remember why. But I do remember I was told.

A: While considering leaving, look on page 66.

A: A hand massaged by a hand.

A: When you look at it that way.

III

I'll never know how to live, will you?

—Alice Notley

POEM IN THE SHAPE OF A TRUMPET

In high school band, back in, well, I won't mention dates because it'll help this seem like a non-memory memory because ugh, memory, I can't really do much with it, so back in or *back then* I used to hold my trumpet up, sitting next to you while you held yours up but you played yours and I didn't at first because I had been playing for awhile for a number of years and the music had gotten harder, but I couldn't tell the teacher because he put me in this spot and besides was in anger management and told me once I stopped trying too hard and set my mouth correctly I would finally put all my air to good use, so I'd just listen to you play the songs a few times and I tried to get them and you were just this kid but you could play, the Irish ballads the jazz the pep songs, they even gave you solos and somehow I had gotten this far, I'm not really sure how especially because of the jazz, and sitting next to you the good player I felt as if I had taken off my training wheels and realized there was never a bike and now, even though I sold my trumpet years ago, I'm still looking for my bike and a little worried that you were it.

THE LAST BARBECUE WE HAD

All through our blackened meat
we watched Angel sniffle like a smile,
no, stare at a tree like a wounded kite, no,
hold a smile that was nothing like a cry.
Nothing we could smile was finer
than Angel frowning, hiccupping, stifling a burp . . .
How we hated the way we swallowed.

Actually, no one had really heard Angel talk before.
At the first cookout she attended we gave her grilled fish
which she tossed on the just-mowed grass because
she wanted it to swim, because she wore purple sandals,
because her character was brilliant!

She probably doesn't eat animals! She probably is just clumsy,
she's rude! urged our friend with the scowl, our dear friend.

At one barbecue
we discovered the way she scooped potato salad on her plate.
Like nobody's princess she held a spoon!
She was the kind of girl who could make it snow in summer.
And she did, not really, but we danced in the fresh whiteness
like it was a piña colada.
Another helping, another scoop, we wanted more Angel!

She barely says anything! Worthless! our friend scowled again,
really never stopped scowling.
No, he was wrong— she says goodbye in French, in Ohio!

Angel, you are a seahorse on a stage!

When could we have another barbecue? When could we see Angel
and be grateful she'd say everything for us, by not saying anything.
No one else could make us feel so uncomfortable, no, unfamiliar.
Yes, that was actually our friend Cyndi who made us feel new, different,
yet how Cyndi was like Angel but not quite as good!
Cyndi how does it feel to be the next best thing!
And being you, Angel,
our *you*, must feel like something!

Our friend couldn't scowl harder, *She blushes and you queen her!*
I should say something now to make you ashamed,
but I couldn't dislike you any more than I do!

And perhaps she's been to only one or two barbecues,
or maybe never came to any at all.
But we needed her—what would we wear, who would we make fish for,
how would we ever have a reason not to scowl?

And at this summer's last golden roast, this last barbecue,
our angry friend appeared to tell us he wasn't attending, to tell us
there wasn't anything left but to wish we were Angel.

Wait for me, wait for me! Angel yelled, *I don't know how this ends!*

Our friend stayed in frown,
took her elbow,
kissed her false eyelashes, held her big toe,
and our precious scowler
fell for Angel, as if
he had loved her once,
as if he had lost her once before—
because it was Angel, because he scowled,
because everyone else's hands held plates.

THE NIGHT BEFORE AN AUBADE

The night before the morning I fall
in love with my neighbor,
he comes over to switch off each light in my house.
Can you ever forgive me? he asks.
Can I ever forgive you? I ask, I don't understand.
No. He repeats, *Can* you *ever forgive me?*
I repeat, *Can you ever forgive me?*
Yes, he answers, unlike sunrise.

I'VE BEEN LEAVING THE LIGHT ON, BUT DON'T COME BY

It didn't do anything wrong.

There is nothing it can be but itself.

What else, it's an ocean. It can't try.

It can't try any harder.

And so I want the sea to just go away.

I ask questions toward it
and must expect myself to answer.
About anything   anything.

I understand,
when I walk on its shores
I'm supposed to know how.

But no,
the sea doesn't work right now— *Leave.   Yes*
you can   yes   yes you can.

Kids on the shore are crying—
It should pull some of them along,
take the strangers I couldn't talk to,
the newlyweds who won't shut up and
their sand-packed heart that should've been a castle,
no, something better than a castle.

They all do what they're only made to.

I need to prove the ocean is what it'll always be,
Go away.
This is how we find out about ourselves.

Yesterday, after a fisher on the beach caught a little shark,
I still stayed inside the waters, and I can't swim.
Shouldn't that say something unlike me?
The sea doesn't even know who I am. How
can I be changed by it when it can't change clothes.

It will never know if I answer.

Go away.

I don't have anywhere to go. The sea
has more options.

LULLABY FOR THE BARRETTE

Your exhaustion doesn't come from holding back
her hair's left part from slipping down the right of her face.
You want everyone to notice her (put that face out in the world!)
but you also want her simply
not to notice if they look at her or don't look.

Some barrettes may get weary
of their click that sets them to match the more important
dress, the handbag, the whole damn event
but you would be a ceaseless accessory to her practiced posture
and eye contact if also to the face that you neatly reveal,
a simple tidying that helps her last from the overture to the parking lot.

You tire over what could happen when you are not
fastened to the hair that longs to drop over one eye
forcing the other to look and be looked at
dividing her into freckles and shadow, into
brow, pout, ass, and what parts hide from names,
into *Why can't this hair lie right!* and *Is this all I can think of?*
then admitting, *these aren't real divisions,* to help order herself.

Yet knowing this doesn't stop the feel of a struggle in her
between bone and moon, cheap jewelry and nude,
between things she thinks of but would never say
and the things she says but only to herself,
between defining her walk and un-naming her kiss
(oh, you've heard what they've called it, why they've left),
trying to place this all with the right blouse,
hoping flipping her hair part will get her out of this.

She wants
a simple inner and outer, a listener a speaker,
clear wins and defeats,
a younger and an older, as she's too old to still hide from a full room—
oh that childish barrette, oh her dead fish name.

Each time unclasped, you might as well be ripped
out and down the length of her hair, splitting its ends, left
with a mouthful to wait on the sink's edge.

      The thought of the day's end is enough for you to droop
            and she has no song to sing nor pajamas to accompany your blue.

What rest could be named after she unclips you?

WHEN THE NEIGHBORHOOD'S ASLEEP

He doesn't look up
because he can't without thinking
those stars,
they're going to fall.
But when he walks through the neighborhood
he likes to know they're up there,
and it's possible they could plummet,
but more possible if
he were to look.

AND THAT IS HOW THE WORLD WORKS

Now that we know how things work, we pack our bags, turn off the TV or lie back
on our side of the bed and ask, *Now what?*
But we still know
how things work and so we know what to do.
Some of us make up stories to share the news,
using giraffes, bats or other creatures for narrative
or wear miniskirts and leap around stages to explain through style and dance.
Some believe never to tell how the world works
and learn how to use swords to prevent others from learning.
Some of us work to get past *I love, I love,* and finally say *you.* Or finally say
You can't dance, or, *There's tartar sauce on your chin.*
Some still buy the same Mich Golden but now
screw more than our husbands or wives.
But once some know how things work,
we just stand in our neighborhood thinking about what to eat,
and watch people tell stories, polish swords, confess and cheat.
The Mounds Bar from the BP or the curry from the corner restaurant
would taste good, but that's how things work, and we know why
it would taste good, besides the cocoa and cumin. And we know why
we curse the burden of knowing the world's workings.
Some cursers make love all day to someone we hate,
and shout to walls, *Figure this out!*
Some who curse knowing the world, punch who we love saying, *This can't be
how the world works!*
And some of us cursers learn
to just watch those in the world who don't know how it works,
and wish we were the ones *goddamn*-ing and *fuck-you*-ing
at the bank tellers, old people, door-slammers, or children
in such a pure unthinking way, a way cursing was made to work.

WORK HARDER

I'm tired of what I can do—
Make lists of things I don't like,
explain the plains of North Dakota
to kill a conversation,
discuss chocolate with strangers.
Other people can
weld, swim, twirl a baton—
I'm tired of this too,
and whatever else there is to do.
What I hate most is what nobody can do.
I work to forget these things.
When I cut into a mango on the right day
I am working.
When I imagine five ways to grin,
I work.
Watching fog, snoring— I call it work,
and it keeps me busy until
I see you walk up Sixth Street.
The things I can't do,
you know every one.
You're just a person.
Tell me what does that mean.
You and I
do what everyone does
and (don't say it) say it has meaning,
say (wait) I have feelings.
What I can do,
I am so unsafe,
is kiss my own hand, which I hope you'll still take—
even though it's been done (we are boring)
done (hang around until tomorrow)
done (tomorrow there's so much to do).

A WAY TO LIVE IN THE NEIGHBORHOOD

I. The Neighborhood

Someone, please
give Sandy what she wants.
The dogs have quit their ill-timed barking,
no one's pulled a turnip this August thought decent,
the chimes no longer accept the wind, and one of us
has stopped the neighborhood watch.
A leaf fell when the others stayed green,
the gutters fall without rain.
It must be her—
she's ended the barbecues. We've seen her dog
swerve from us. She only looks at our blisterless paint,
its smooth gaze only watches us.
What does she know? What does she want?
Sandy, how does it feel
to have everything figured out?

II. Sandy

I'm suddenly from Spain,   I'm the Christmas lights unhung,

        I'm landing on their lawns in a hot-air balloon,
                        I'm their choirgirl who's cut out the tune.

What do my neighbors really want to know?

Here is the story of their robes falling in wrong windows.
Here is the story of borrowed milk gone to good use.

I see there is no difference in happy endings.

I used to call from my porch

until I realized I had to.

I see no one took in the stray cat I positioned on the playground.

My barbecue grill is simply past scrubbing.

I know too much. I am never disappointed

and will glean these chimes until I really know

what not to want.

III. A Neighbor

If I were not a neighbor, I'd still choose
to live here.
I'd have a fence
because it wouldn't offend. I wouldn't
have a fence because I'd have nothing to defend.

You know
that cat can stray forever.

Sandy, I do not know how
to be a neighbor. Let's disappoint each other. Let's
get the neighbors talking. We will anyway. I want to come over.
Disappointment doesn't wait.

IV. Another Neighbor

Dear houses around me . . . hello neighbors . . . excuse me—
beings and bodies in homes
near mine and close enough
to walk to with a warm kettle,

       someone to compare an enemy to,

royalty of the court of small

talk, meat

of the gossip,

hosts of the borrowed,

makers of want,

mistaken owners of trees.

Neighbors and your neighbors

convince me you're not neighbors

              without packing up.

You residents of tiny disappointment

and fragile potlucks,

what can we get each other not to say?

A PLEA THAT'S NOTHING LIKE SAMUEL'S

Everyone has left,
and those who have not left this town
know each other in a way I wouldn't.
Samuel, whoever he is,
pleaded for Laura who was just waiting
for him to drive after her under-packed truck.
Dan has the number of everyone
who wants him to stay in town.
Louise told Steve
she'd never wait for anyone but him.
And he stayed— who would do such a thing?
Please, someone's lying.

Please, please . . . I want to leave.

It may matter
that none of these people are my friends.
None of my friends would stay.
I, like them, always knew how to leave
those who wished me well.
I always thought a see-ya barbecue
and a bright future without each other
were the way things worked.

Someone come back and ask me to stay
so I can feel good about getting my tires rotated
and leave.

You were the last to leave town
and sent me a postcard with cows,
saying you took a boat to get away for good
in your disappointment with my willingness
to wish you well (when you said you might go).

And still, you managed to make it work
when you realized it was a whale-watching tour boat.

I am left here—
I see cows every day.
Here I am left
to become a better person or,
more importantly, to think about how well
I'm doing among the sorry people
who stayed or pleaded.

ANOTHER FAREWELL SONG

Oh music, you can give it and take it.

We thought you'd make us unlike fences,
would give us bodies to swim dirty seas or lives like the old trees,
give us wars and banners for the wars, loves like war, banners against love,
a love against wars—
give us oars to paddle and paddle, hit land and waddle, stamp
right up to the kiss, the storm, the tower and ring the bell.

Again, again—

We listened and took off terrycloth.
We didn't know how to moan. We listened. We didn't know
what was better than the moans.

                          We couldn't stop yelping, *I'm not ready for this!*

 Whispering, *so this so this   so this is what it's like.*

We would be firm and shiny after the song.
                          Better said, we'd be fit astronauts ready for moon sex.
Oh that's what we should've said, should have been.
                    Of course, we can't remember which song that was.

Once during the music we were low,
we were ugly-kid low, nobody's eyes would've given us birth. Toads. Heads like shovels.
But we couldn't turn it off— would we feel worse, were we down before the songs?
And so we kept listening. We hoped to leap.

We were gonna say

       I'm taking the last cookie, the kids, the hammer.
       I'll take it with hot sauce!   I'll take on the whale.
       I'm quitting this toilet and moving on to become a star.

—all of it all of it just after the song.

The turntable was turning
and the best thing we could think of was to turn it backwards.

Hit me Jack, I'm the road.

You'd say,   *Let go. There must be a letting go.*

                            There is no go to let.

We've heard the song about souls. We've heard the song about paper souls.
We listened, folded, folded and folded but we just made crumpled trash.

We've heard the one about truck driving and making it. We've heard
one sung with wit, one with rage and wit.

We can't do anything but list.

            We listen and listen until they're just songs again.
The old trees are just standing luck.

Nobody wants to think of the ways songs never end?

Even if there's no reason,
no need to play music during dinner with meat,
we still bite. Sometimes down on our blind, fixed tongues.
We still cut and section our lives with refrains.
We can't have a gala without them. We can't put the babies to sleep.

Play the one about the lonely who get the courage to admit their loneliness
or the one about the lonely who one day die lonely.
One more time let's hear of the roses that ruin the raindrops.

Babies, go back to bed.

And while there may not actually be any sad gals
play their tune anyway.

Yes the gals will keep waiting for their love to lose its lyrics—
but the gals always find their way home.

**CHARLIE WANTS TO KNOW *WHAT'S GONNA HAPPEN NEXT*?
CHARLIE, LET ME KNOW, TOO!**

When I say, "It's gonna be okay," sometimes Charlie gets angry.
"You don't know!" he says. But he doesn't want me to know. He may not
know this at the time. But he'd hear it in my voice, if I believed what I said.
Then he'd know what was gonna be. Listen, if I sounded confident, it would be terrible.
This would prove there was a way to know. There would come a time when I'd
say, "It's gonna be okay," and just shouldn't have said it. Unless the whole mess was my
fault. Yes, he would know what was true, then, but in a quite different way.

Some days it's all Charlie wants to hear.

I may seem harmless. I point out a thing or two and have no demands.
Not true. I have all sorts of questions.
Favorite word? Greatest fear? On second thought?

POEM IN THE SHAPE OF WHAT STICKS

Nobody saw me blow my gum out
onto the sidewalk, but it still makes me
feel tough. On the street,
I see a white-haired lady walking her black lab,
then a guy in corduroy pants. Both look
at their reflections in the muffin shop window.
When I go by, nobody sees
that I don't look for me. I'm not even hungry.

But there are anybodies— the someones I don't see,
the someone up in the apartment with the
green-curtained window, the person that will step on my gum.

I will be stuck to the bottom of a clog or wingtip.
A red sneaker worn by a woman
walking to the gym. She's feeling feisty, she hates
being a nurse, and now every left step sticks.
It's when she draws the blood, searches
for the best vein, that gets her— she often still misses.
When she walks past the muffin shop,
she doesn't stop for breakfast,
and when she looks ahead she sees me, nobody.

LONELINESS, BUT NOTHING REALLY LIKE IT

Lately I've had this constant feeling   of feeling like myself
Feeling like me fills my days   That tree I can't name fills my days
                                        Someone's shirt is stuck in that tree
I am full of strangers   I wonder which one is you

Your sad face is a net   My sad face is a persistent fish—

    I'm beginning to understand how things get caught

Watching the tree   I smell an air that has no season
                              which feels like me whenever I want

Anyone anyone   nature doesn't have shoulders   stop leaning your head

                         I feel this   no   I fill you

Oh I don't want to get quiet now   don't want to look up at the tree I can't name
I want it to fill me   or think of a name and let the shirt go   instead of me

Lonely lonely shoulders   I don't care who you are—
why do you not come back for that shirt   how do you?

Anyone anyone
                   I am bursting
How it started   I don't want to find out

Under your buttons   silly strangers   you have
what I need   so I don't want to know you
One of you is cracking my window   one of you already took down the whiskey
How does it feel to know me

My stranger   my little fish   your frown undresses me—
                                        I could have my way
Heavy with buttons   with no dinner guest for me to inspire
                                        thinner and thinner I get

There is more than one way to walk around me

THE NEIGHBORHOOD OUTSIDE OF THIS ONE

Maybe that's where all the deer have gone.
I like to think I sent them there, pushing them out
by accusing that they need us
to put them in stories and painted grass,
give them pets, comb their fur, turn to each other
and comb each other's hair, our suddenly golden hair,
while they run away when we are deep in each other.
We need them back when our lovers leave.

Yes, that other neighborhood is where I'm sure they've gone.

You don't know for sure, my neighbors say.

But I do, so do they.

Deer are supposed to run through these parts of town.
There's a forest somewhere out there. Out there, out there.

On second thought, maybe they'd add something.
I bet that other neighborhood runs after deer with heart-shaped treats.
                    Second thoughts, you run too quickly.

Deer, maybe I have a hard time letting go of you too
but it's not because I want to admire the grace of the bend to the berries
and the way this move makes us want to touch the tall grass
and ask ourselves for secret forgiveness.
Ugh, now I talk to you just like my neighbors would.

I know, I don't trust myself either. I know I know—
not even what I just said! I know I *know* people don't actually pet deer.

Maybe it would be a
                     Let us in!

                                    Let us out!
situation, if the neighborhoods met
                     but each side would consider themselves the winner. *I know you want in.*

If I went over to that other neighborhood perhaps they'd say
they never had deer— *What, and you do?*
We did we did, and I sent them away. I don't remember them
but I had something to do with it.   Don't touch my hair!

Then maybe these outsiders would say, *Don't worry, people are forgiving.*
Maybe this could be true, after all— but what fun is that?

I stay in my neighborhood hoping one of us will say,
You chased the deer out! I'll never forgive you!
                          just enough times so I can still comfortably stay.
I couldn't leave with that kind of success.

Or, do I stay until someone says, *I forgive you?*
                          What could they get me to feel? I fear they would.

If I could get inside their forgiveness I could see if it's the kind that's like
giving a bouquet from a garden unintended for cut flowers.

But I can't get in. They haven't forgiven me.
They look at each other, not the lack of deer.

That morning with the deer, while sitting in your breakfast nook, that was me! Me. I took
that away. You must miss them.

Deer are just deer. There's only one way to disappoint them—

I'll stay to figure out the other ways. Oh, and a backup plan to these ways, too.

DANCING IN SHORTY'S BAR

I am such a loser and will always
be alone, is a phrase many have
said to a friend or whispered
under the covers of a queen-sized bed.
I wish someone would stop me
in the street and say,

I'm a sweet sweet loser! Or
sing from a dark stage, *I am beautiful when I'm alone.*

For every reason tonight
I am dancing to "Mustang Sally" in
a bar with the locals of Troy, Montana.
A tough, tan woman sings backup,
smacks her thigh with tambourine. Her voice
cannot be heard through the blues.
I feel like I am outside in the snow
shooting blanks at a train passing midnight by;
the shots bring out drinkers and dancers,
who listen to me make noise, their lone bodies ring.
We howl as the train takes us
deep in the muscle of night.

Yes everyone in this bar dances foolishly,
midnight breaks all standards.
No one wants to go home to them,
especially now when tambourine Sally hands
me her mic, I rise to the stage like smoke
from a foreign cigarette held between
fingertips, burning quickly towards flesh.
We are alone,

I belt and hold until
the band plays below me.
We are so damn uncool. We are
so lonely we do not know
how to ask ourselves to dance.

A REFRAIN, SUNG ONCE, TO HERSELF

One day, I worry, you will tell me
everything I've told you.

What do you have to say for yourself?

Nothing.

Did you think I wouldn't be listening?

I don't know.

There is a moon born every time I say *alone*
and tonight its light has left me sore.
I can see my breath, and I wonder about everything—
how I'm going to get home,
how to answer *What's your story?*
how to ask you to walk with me.

"Listen, listen," the moon, my polished child, says, "On your knees."
I put my ear to the road.
I cut my hand on street glass.
I hear a sigh, I hear a step, I see you
ignoring the shadows, walking towards me.
I couldn't say just anything.

RUBY, GIVE LEO ONE MORE CHANCE

I.

Maybe there is no difference between
the stories about kisses and the kisses about stories.
If I were a mother I could turn to my baby's screams,
tell her to use that strength for when she feels this way.
But all the babies are where they're supposed to be—
things don't just happen and not happen.

There's not a lot of difference
between Leo and Ruby staying in love or not.
I know I'm wrong, but I want to start somewhere.
I am also not wrong, and here is when I start
unbuttoning my coat while my other hand tries to zip up.
It's better than saying they'll work it out.
The way my lovers leave is like things just happening.
Take the stories with you.

II.

Ruby loves Leo enough, but she likes to suggest leaving him.
Ruby is just waiting for Leo to leave her again.
Leo doesn't know why anyone bothers.
Leo looks for new stories about beauty—
A stranger with a sty instead of a wink,
ugly cries, big thighs, barns with chipped paint.
Short hair instead of long hair. Ruby cuts her hair.
At this point, and forever, Ruby and Leo could be married only to each other.
And, again, I'm wrong.
Leo notices me, and Ruby notices us.
Ruby is not going to let Leo leave with Chubby.
This dog, their dog Chubby, is waiting to be walked.

Don't laugh, but I wonder if this sweet dog
is their glue, then there's a shrug of shoulders
and a baby is conceived— that's life. True?
I didn't want to be in this story,
and I can't stop looking at Ruby's growing stomach.

Give me a minute, I can tell you a little more.

It started growing the day after Ruby's face turned pale,
the day Leo explained barns to me.
I don't even know these people well.

What do I want them to convince me of? I wish
I was making this up.

III.

I don't know what everyone is talking about, I don't agree. You can know a person.

You can watch someone all night and know his pause.
Be introduced to the right candidate for the job.
You can tell who is here every night.
You can tell who never weeps. Let's not use weep.

In the beginning I enjoyed you more than I thought I would.

You can know a person too well. You can know a story.
You can feel nothing at all.

I can walk up to a stranger and, and I—
who cares what I could say.
This isn't about talking to strangers.

It's not so hard.
This person cuts me off. That person avoids me. She flinches
when I say his name but even more when I try not to.
I don't want to look at you one day and lie.

Don't think I've gotten soft.
Leo wants, "I know," and I'm not going to say it.
A lover wants me to watch him leave with arms around I don't know who.
I know exactly what I'm moved by. This is the first sentence of my story with you.

PACKAGES UNDER OUR CONTROL

I.

The neighbors tell him that after packaging a package, they prep their package. They talk to the package. *Keep it together!* They yell. *Own your opening!* Afraid to let it go. They explain box cutters, untying, powerful yanks. They warn the package of others' dread or impatience that may come before it does. They mail it and claim it a route. Sometimes they package the package, saying, *See, this is what it's like to be packaged!* hoping the package can hear through the packaging that envelops it.

Don't open so easily! Explaining surprise. The package may be inside the surprise or outside of it. Surprise may come before surprise. As in, one could be surprised to get the package but not by what's in the package. Or, maybe so! But, oh dear, if the surprise is what's inside, is it the contents or the sight of the contents? The space between the contents and the hand about to touch the contents. Between the hand that touches the contents and the one that will touch your face.

Now we're talking about longing. This really wasn't planned.

Some senders open their package before sending it. They look at its insides, now parts. No package, no way to tell how it's going to turn out, other than repackaging it.

II.

He lives on the third floor. She lives at garden level. Tonight, he put a package outside her window and went home.

In the morning, it's hard to name. She wants to tell him what it was like to find his package, to open it. That space between morning and this morning.

There is something he'd like to tell her. Of the only night he couldn't sleep and wanted to ask so many questions. Has she ever fallen up? What do wasps do that honeybees can't? When is the moment when ice isn't ice? He tried to fall asleep like he thought everyone did, on his back, stretched out but muscles relaxed. He counted sheep and then they watched him hold it together like everyone else must. Low breathing with light snore. Sticking to his back or sides, body always straight, always in the shape of someone sleeping. But, delighted, in the morning, he woke to find himself in the shape of something like a four.

She tells him, yes, it was something like that. Tonight she'll fall asleep in the shape of a four, hoping anything but an equation will come to her in sleep.

SANDY'S LIST OF SOLUTIONS

I should've lied less and said *I confess,*

then everyone would think I slip them secrets.

I should've worried about my lack of stories.

I should've acknowledged machines.

I should've left a scarf in all the doorways.

We could've been friends.

I dropped the spare keys along the way.

They're going to notice I never mention God.

The oldest neighbor in the neighborhood said just be happy

to be one of the locked-out.

I should've been as lonely as I said I was.

Wet lottery tickets littered on the walking path to work,

the fingernails that pierced the apples I want to buy—

these dirty moons, is this all I have? The images

that I'm to make something lovely with—

Fruit marked with rejection is supposed to be enough to live for?

I could live next door to disappointment.

I should make an apple pie, or just a cobbler. Oh neighbors!

It is easy to try hard. It's easy to make sense of things. I never want

to give in to the stories.

Damn, those women know how to attract them. I can't stop

eavesdropping on it all wrong.

The oldest neighbor in the neighborhood said, I will be happy, one day

(day one!), just to see all those who look better than I or, really, just look.

ACKNOWLEDGMENTS

The following poems have appeared or will appear in these publications:

"We Like Steve and Louise's Love," "Poem in the Shape of a Trumpet," "Joy," "Another Farewell Song," published in The Poetry Center of Chicago's 2009 Juried Reading Series e-chapbook by Plastique Press.

"Poem in the Shape of a Trumpet," and "Ruby, Give Leo One More Chance," *Barn Owl Review*.

"Storm's A'Comin," and "Neighbor Curse," *storySouth*.

"A Way to Live in the Neighborhood," *The Laurel Review*.

"A Refrain, Sung Once, to Herself," *32 Poems*.

"I Have Been in More Uncomfortable Situations than This," *DIAGRAM*.

"Apology to Meditation," *Mid-American Review*.

"His List of Solutions," *Colorado Review*.

"The Women Wear Black," *Best New Poets*, 2005.

"The Women Wear Black," and "Work Harder," *Third Coast*.

"All My Friends' Barbecues Need Attending," *Greensboro Review*.

"Dancing in Shorty's Bar," *South Dakota Review*.

Thank you to the following writers who contributed to the existence of this book before, during, or after its completion:

Mark Halliday, Sharmila Voorakkara, Darrell Spencer, Jill Allyn Rosser, Jonathan Johnson, Christopher Howell, Nance van Winckel, Jennifer Reid, Lyn Canterbury, Jason Olsen, Scott Poole, Renée Roehl, Ashley Seitz Kramer, David Bruzina, Tracey Knapp, Beth Thompson, Daniel Koltonski, Angela Mazakis, Sara Pennington, Emily Zaborniak, and David Dodd Lee.

A special thanks to Megan Lobsinger for her help, and to whom this book is also dedicated.

Many thanks to Ohio University's English Department for their generous time and support that allowed the completion of this book.

And thanks and love to Kent Shaw, who supported the book at the right time.

Carrie Oeding is a native of Minnesota. She has taught at Ohio University and The University of Houston. She received her M.F.A. from Eastern Washington University and her Ph.D. from Ohio University, where she was awarded the Claude Kantner Fellowship.